A

· G · U · I · D · E ·

T O

PLAYING

David Elkan

 Melbourne House Publishers

Published in the United Kingdom by:
Melbourne House (Publishers) Ltd.,
Church Yard,
Tring, Hertfordshire HP23 5LU.
ISBN 0 86161 161 6

Published in Australia by:
Melbourne House (Australia) Pty. Ltd.,
70 Park Street,
South Melbourne, Victoria, 3205.

Printed in Hong Kong by Colorcraft Ltd.

DCBA9876543210

Contents

Playing The Hobbit 1
Part 1: Through the Round Green Door 3
Starting Out 3
The Inglish Language 3
Moving Around 4
Further Inglish Lessons 5
Weights and Measures 7
Collecting Treasure 8
Doors and Passageways 8
Other Characters 9
Thorin 9
Gandalf 10
Mapping 10
Your Score 12
Part 2: The Hobbit Help Section 13
Section 1: Setting Out 13
Section 2: The Misty Mountains 14
Section 3: The Goblins' Caves 15
Section 4: Beorn's House 16
Section 5: The Elven King's Halls 17
Section 6: Long Lake 18
Section 7: The Dragon's Desolation 18
Part 3: A Tourist's Guide to Wilderland 19
L1: Beorn's house 20
L2: The bewitched gloomy place 21
L3: A big cavern with torches along the walls 22
L4: A bleak barren land that was once green 23
L5: The cellar where the king keeps his barrels of wine 24
L6: A comfortable tunnel like hall 26
L7: A dark dungeon in the elven king's halls 27
L8: The dark stuffy passage 28
L9: The dark winding passage 31
L10: The east bank of a black river 32
L11: The elven king's great halls 33
L12: An elvish clearing with levelled ground and logs 34
L13: The empty place 35

L14: The forest 36
L15: A forest of tangled smothering trees 37
L16: The forest road 38
L17: The forest road 39
L18: Forestriver 40
L19: The front gate of the Lonely Mountain 41
L20: The gate to Mirkwood 42
L21: A gloomy empty land with dreary hills ahead 43
L22: The goblins' dungeon 44
L23: The great river 46
L24: The green forest 47
L25: The halls where the dragon sleeps 48
L26: A hard dangerous path in the Misty Mountains 49
L27: A hidden path with trolls' footprints 50
L28: Inside the goblins' gate 51
L29: A large dry cave which is quite comfortable 52
L30: A little steep bay, still and quiet, with an overhanging cliff . 53
L31: The Lonely Mountain 54
L32: Long Lake 55
L33: The mountains 56
L34: A narrow path 57
L35: A narrow dangerous path 58
L36: A narrow place with a dreadful drop into a dim valley 59
L37: Outside goblins' gate 60
L38: A place of black spiders 61
L39: Rivendell 62
L40: The ruins of the town of Dale 63
L41: The running river 64
L42: A smooth straight passage 65
L43: A strong river 66
L44: The treeless opening 67
L45: The trolls' cave 68
L46: The trolls' clearing 69
L47: The waterfall 70
L48: The west bank of a black river 71
L49: The west side of Ravenhill 72
L50: A wooden town in the middle of Long Lake 73
Index of Listed Locations 75

Foreword by the authors of the Hobbit Adventure

This book is a solution to successfully playing the Hobbit on your micro. As such we think it would be a valuable aid to those people who have not as yet completed the adventure or to those who want to find a quick way through.

With most adventures a book such as this would thoroughly spoil the adventure for those who are playing it. However, because the Hobbit does not have just one right method to completing the adventure, we feel that the book does not detract from the fun that one can have playing it.

In many cases the solutions offered are not those which we would have chosen, but then everyone will eventually have his own preferred 'solution', the point is though that they work.

This is perhaps where this book's greatest value lies. It proves that the adventure can be completed and gives some idea of what can be accomplished with Inglish and Animaction.

To any reader of this book we would say don't ever underestimate the Hobbit. Keep trying variations on the methods shown here and you will discover just how versatile the Hobbit really is.

Playing The Hobbit

This guide is designed to help you to play and solve 'The Hobbit', one of the most popular and most sophisticated games currently available for a home computer.

The book is divided into three parts, each giving away slightly more than the previous one, allowing the game to be played at your own chosen level.

Part one contains general ideas and hints on what you should look out for while playing the game. Part two adds to the hints already given in the game by using the HELP command, and should allow you to work out your own solutions to the problems you encounter. Part three is in the form of a full reference section listing the locations, their exits, and any other commands you may need to use to pass certain obstacles.

No two games are alike, and this guide will help you to discover more about The Hobbit each time you play.

Part One

Through the Round Green Door

This part gives ideas and strategies which you will need to use while playing The Hobbit. A summary of the rules of Inglish is also included, but for a fuller introduction you should read the booklet supplied with the game. There are also sections on carrying objects, searching locations, mapping and hints on playing the game to help you tackle problems you may meet.

STARTING OUT

Having loaded The Hobbit you are faced with a motionless title page. You press a key and the game begins — the screen is divided into two and your current location, Bilbo's home, is described to you.

The top part of the screen shows information about what is happening in the game and descriptions of the places you arrive at and the things you see there. Many locations have pictures (not on the BBC cassette version) to give you an idea of your surroundings, and these are shown here when you first enter the location or use the LOOK command.

The lower part of the screen is where you type your instructions to the computer, telling it what you want to do. If something you type in doesn't make sense to the computer it will tell you here.

THE INGLISH LANGUAGE

For those familiar with adventure games, Inglish is a powerful extension to the usual two word 'verb-then-noun' type of input. For others, it gives the chance to instruct the computer using simple English sentences. The rules of the language are given in the booklet supplied with the game, but are summarised below.

As in English each sentence must contain a verb. The simplest sentences will be a verb only:

RUN
WAIT
LOOK

Adverbs can also be included to describe how you perform an action, but are not essential to the meaning of the sentence:

RUN QUICKLY
KILL VICIOUSLY

Some verbs, however, will require a noun:

OPEN THE DOOR
TAKE THE KEY

If the game uses adjectives to describe an object, then you can also use them. Adjectives normally come before the noun, as they would in English:

OPEN THE GREEN DOOR
TAKE THE LARGE KEY

In longer sentences the order of the different parts is not important. Both

KILL THE GOBLIN VICIOUSLY WITH THE SWORD
WITH THE SWORD VICIOUSLY KILL THE GOBLIN

amount to exactly the same instruction and both are equally valid.

Prepositions such as with, under, on, off usually come before the noun:

ATTACK WITH THE SWORD
PICK UP THE TREASURE

Although in some cases, when it would sound more natural, they can be put after the noun:

TURN THE LIGHT ON
PICK THE SWORD UP

In general if the command that you wish to type makes sense in English, then its Inglish form would be exactly the same: To take the golden key you would enter TAKE THE GOLDEN KEY, and so on.

MOVING AROUND

Each location is described to you with its visible exits listed — these can be in any of the eight directions of the compass, as well as up and down.

4

There are several ways by which you can actually move:

1: Enter the direction, or just its abbreviation, in which you want to move —

eg EAST or just E
SOUTHWEST or SW

2: If one of the other characters has just left, you can follow —

eg Supposing Gandalf has just gone east, you can then enter FOLLOW GANDALF and you too would go east.

3: To go through an entrance such as a door, you should first make sure that the door is open, before typing —

GO THROUGH DOOR

If you know which direction the door is in, you can simply type that direction —

eg Had you been told that there is a door to the east, you could then enter EAST or E and you would go through the door.

A useful advantage is that you can LOOK THROUGH doors and windows to see where they lead to.

FURTHER INGLISH LESSONS

Using Inglish you can shorten commands almost as much as you can expand them.

When specifying a direction to move in:

E could be used for EAST
N for NORTH
SE for SOUTHEAST

and so on.

The word GO is not needed before a direction to move in, and neither is RUN. A simple sentence could just be:

E instead of GO EAST

Adverbs are generally not needed:

RUN EAST QUICKLY could be shortened to just E

Adjectives can also be dropped as long as this would not lead to confusion between two or more objects:

TAKE THE CURIOUS MAP can become TAKE MAP with no change in meaning.

If, however, you found two similar keys, one red and one golden, just typing TAKE KEY would not tell the computer which one you wanted to take, and you would need to be more specific by typing TAKE RED KEY. The same would apply if you were carrying two similar objects and wanted to drop one of them, or you were faced with two doors and could go through either.

The word AND can be used to join separate sentences, but when using it bear in mind that you will do things no more quickly — other characters will carry on with their own affairs in between your commands.

An example of this could be:

DROP RED KEY AND TAKE SWORD

If, when you drop the key, Gandalf takes the sword himself, by the time the computer gets to the TAKE SWORD part of your instruction, the sword is no longer there!

Using ALL works in the same way. Entering TAKE ALL has the same effect as if you had picked up each of the objects separately — the other characters continue moving while you are picking up each object.

Punctuation has the same result as if you had used AND to separate a sentence, and you should therefore be similarly careful:

EAST AND NORTH AND DOWN

is the same as

EAST, NORTH, DOWN.

The only limit made to the amount you type is that it must not be longer than 128 characters at a time.

ALL, EVERYTHING and EXCEPT can be used as they would be in English:

> TAKE ALL EXCEPT THE SWORD
> EAT EVERYTHING
> DROP ALL KEYS EXCEPT THE RED ONE

All these are valid.

When talking about two objects, AND can be used:

> DROP THE RED AND GOLDEN KEYS
> TAKE THE LAMP AND ROPE OUT OF THE BARREL

One point that must be noted is that the word RUN does not allow you to nominate a direction. RUN is used to get out of a location fast and therefore The Hobbit responds by taking the quickest way out, despite any direction you have added.

WEIGHTS AND MEASURES

During the game you will find many objects, some useful, some not so useful. A few will have magical properties to enable you to overcome specific problems. Others such as ropes, maps and food will help you with the mundane task of getting around in Wilderland.

As Bilbo, a Hobbit, you have no magical powers of your own and being small there is a limit to the amount that you can carry. Some objects weigh more than others, and you will not be able to go on collecting things indefinitely. Many objects will be too heavy to carry at all — in this event you could ask one of the other characters to take it for you providing it is not too heavy for them also. Picking up a cupboard will, for instance, be too heavy for both Bilbo and Thorin, while Gandalf is rarely with you long enough to carry anything usefully. Be careful, though, if another character cannot take something that you ask him to, he will simply ignore your instruction.

In some circumstances you yourself may be too heavy, should you wish one of the other characters to carry you. In these cases you will have to drop something that you are carrying. As a guide to what can be discarded, objects such as keys usually have one use in opening a particular door and can be safely left behind once you have used them.

Fighting will weaken you and make you less able to pick up even the lightest objects, so eating any food you have with you will help you to regain lost strength.

COLLECTING TREASURE

A few of the objects you will need are hidden and must be located before they can be taken. It will often help to move large objects in order to help find smaller ones — something too heavy to take itself can often be opened or moved, revealing something smaller within or underneath.

Liquids can be drunk from their source, but in order to carry them you will need some sort of container. If the container breaks then the liquid may be lost when it spills out, so care should be taken.

Be careful when trying to break one object using another. Attempting to break down a door using a sword may result in the sword breaking rather than the door. Objects should be used for their intended purpose, in this case the sword for fighting. Some objects are fragile and may shatter if you drop them, so extra care should be taken with these.

You do not have to be carrying an object in order to be able to use it — the object just needs to be in the same place as you are. You cannot, however, use an object if one of the other characters is carrying it — they will not give up their possessions lightly. One way of taking something from another character would be simply to ask for it. For instance, if Thorin is carrying the map you could enter SAY TO THORIN 'GIVE ME THE MAP'. If he chooses to do so he will then give you the map.

DOORS AND PASSAGEWAYS

Many doors are locked and will need a special key to open them, while others you may find open. Some will close by themselves while others still must be broken down. In general doors are there to be used and will lead you through to another part of the game.

Some doors may be hidden, so they must be found before they can be used. If you can move something, do, and you may discover a hidden door or passage leading away.

You may not have the strength yourself to break down a locked door, and should remember that the other characters may be stronger than you are more able to do the job. Co-operation with the other characters is the key to a successful adventure.

Look carefully around each location, as the way ahead may not always be obvious. Before swimming a river, look across to the other side to see what may await you. Look through a door or window if you are unsure as to where it leads, and use the HELP command as often as you need to.

OTHER CHARACTERS

While playing don't always take the other characters too seriously. What they say to you is often of little relevance to the game, while Thorin's singing can be safely ignored! Gandalf and Thorin will be the two characters you are likely to meet the most during the game; Thorin should follow you through much of the adventure. You will also encounter others — many friendly while others are not, so it is important that you do not attack on sight. The book of The Hobbit will be a good guide as to which characters mean you harm, but a goblin slicing at your arm is certainly not showing a sign of friendship!

You can fight bare handed   Inglish will assume this if you do not specify a weapon — but you will be far more capable of doing damage when using a weapon such as a sword. Thorin and Gandalf should not, however, be attacked as both are far stronger than you and quite capable of killing you.

When talking to the other characters make sure that what you want to say makes sense — if it doesn't then your instructions will be ignored. If you are confident that the instruction will work, but if the character you speak to subbornly says 'No', then repeat the instruction until the character complies. Persistency will always help.

THORIN

All being well, Thorin should follow you through at least the first half of the game. After this he becomes a nuisance and can be left behind.

Remember though that he will only follow you when he can see you. If for some reason he cannot, Thorin may wander off on his own.

GANDALF

Gandalf the wizard sadly lacks much of the wisdom of the character in the book, The Hobbit. His moves tend to be fairly random as are the things he says to you. One of Gandalf's habits is to take an object, ask what it is, and then return it — strange behaviour indeed! He is, however, one of the strongest characters you will meet and quite capable of lifting things which you are unable to, or fighting, unarmed, opponents that are too strong for you to attack.

MAPPING

Learning to find your way around Wilderland will be one of the most important parts of your adventure, and designing a map could help you greatly.

A simple, standard way to map an adventure game would just be to draw a diagram of the links between locations:

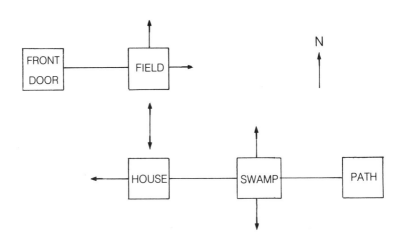

This is fine as long as the directions involved are simple north, south, east and west links. When applied to a game like The Hobbit, this becomes more difficult:

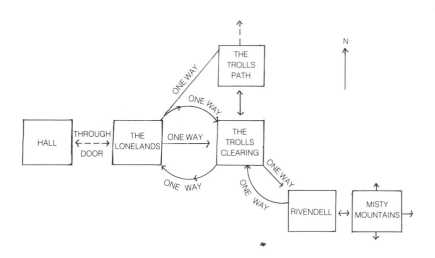

Mapping an area such as the Misty Mountains or the Goblins' Caves would be virtually impossible using this method, and some other way of mapping Wilderland will need to be used.

One method would be to make up a matrix, or table, of directions between locations. Rows could be places travelled from, columns place travelled to, and on the table would be the directions themselves. Draw the grid on squared paper, and each time you arrive at a new location add its name to the 'from' and 'to' parts of the grid together with the direction you travelled in to get there.

Laid out in this way, the first few locations would appear as follows:

		TO						
		COMFORTABLE HALL	THE LONELANDS	THE TROLLS CLEARING	RIVENDELL	THE MISTY MOUNTAIN	THE TROLLS PATH	THE TROLLS CAVE
F	COMFORTABLE HALL		E					
	THE LONELANDS	W		E/N				
R	THE TROLLS CLEARING		SW		SE	N		
O	RIVENDELL			W		E		
M	THE MISTY MOUNTAIN				W			
	THE TROLLS PATH			S				N
	THE TROLLS CAVE						S	

Although complicated to use at first, this method is ideal for mapping many of the very complicated areas of Wilderland. As you will quickly find out when playing the game, paths twist and turn, and going in one direction then back the opposite way will not always take you back to where you started from.

YOUR SCORE

While playing you need not visit every location or solve every puzzle in order to succeed at the adventure. The game can be 'solved' having mastered only around 50%-60%, but in order to improve your score you should try to solve as many problems as possible. The percentage is not increased uniformly as you go through the game, but jumps in steps of 2.5% or more as you reach certain places or perform certain actions. Develop your own routes through Wilderland in order to take in as many locations as possible and increase your score.

Part Two

The Hobbit Help Section

This section expands on the hints already given in the game when using HELP, and in some cases where HELP gives no clue at all hints are given here. The game has been divided into seven sections, each of which you will need to pass through in order to complete the adventure.

Only those locations where you are likely to need help are listed. The long location names are used to described the locations in most cases — the game gives you these descriptions when you first enter a location or when you use the LOOK command.

In cases where several hints are given, a simple code has been used to discourage you from looking ahead to the further hints straight away. The code used is a simple letter substitution:

A B C D E F G H I J K L M N O P Q R S T U V W X Y Z
C D E F G H I J K L M N O P Q R S T U V W X Y Z A B

If, after using this section, you still find yourself stranded at a particular location, you can look up the location in part three, where more complete solutions are given.

SECTION 1:
Setting Out

From the comfortable hall in Bilbo's house you will embark on your adventure. The wooden chest in the hall is the one into which you must put the dragon's treasure at the end of the game.

H1:   A comfortable tunnel like hall

HELP: You're doing fine.
HINT: Go through the green door!

13

H2: The trolls' clearing

HELP: Wait for the new day dawning.
HINT: You can't wait around here . . .
FURTHER HINT: Vtqnnu vwtp vq uvqpg kp fcankijv.

H3: A hidden path with trolls' footprints

HELP: A trolls' door needs a trolls' key.
HINT: A trolls' key comes from a trolls' clearing.
FURTHER HINT: Qpeg fca jcu fcypgf tgvwtp vq igv vjg mga.

H4: Rivendell

HELP: Elves are good at reading symbols.
HINT: What could Elrond read that you can't?
FURTHER HINT: Vta vjg ocr.
EXTRA HINT: Wait a while and see what happens.

SECTION 2:
The Misty Mountains

The paths in this region are designed to deceive and confuse, leading round in circles or nowhere at all. If you do not follow a definite route you may find yourself lost, but careful mapping will be rewarded . . .

H5: A hard dangerous path in the misty mountains

HELP: You're doing fine.
HINT: Search around, but don't get lost.

H6: A large dry cave which is quite comfortable

HELP: You're doing fine.
HINT: The small insignificant crack looks quite significant.

SECTION 3:

The Goblins' Caves

The goblins' caves consist of many passages which twist, turn and double back frequently. Very careful mapping of the passages will help you to work out routes through the caves — several are suggested in part three, but these are only a guide and many different routes can be devised.

Tactically, it is actually beneficial to be captured by a goblin, as going through the dungeon may lead you to something which will be of use later in the game. The goblins themselves appear to move in fixed patterns and can easily be killed using the short sword, but this is of little use as their numbers do not diminish and by the time you have killed one goblin, another may have entered and will capture you. In some cases a goblin may have the strength to kill you.

The caves are the home of Gollum, keeper of the magic ring which you must retrieve if your adventure is to be a success. As a warning, it is best not to answer Gollum's riddles unless you are completely confident of your answer. Gollum will strangle you if you give him the wrong answer. If Gollum follows, asking his riddles, you can easily kill him using the short sword. This is often the best course of action.

Using the golden ring:

Once you have recovered the magical golden ring from the caves, bear in mind that its powers are limited and only last for a short while. If you wish to remain invisible for a long period of time, you should WEAR RING every three of four moves. While you are wearing the ring, Thorin will be unable to see you and as a result will not follow you, so it is important not to use the ring until you are safely clear of the caves. If you do not do this you may find yourself inside the dungeon without Thorin and with no hope of escape.

Thorin:

Once you have found the ring and escaped from the goblins' caves Thorin is of little use to you, and becomes more of a hindrance than a help. To leave him behind at any time just wear the golden ring and walk off — Thorin won't be able to see in which direction you went and as a result will not follow. However, to complete 100% you must bring Thorin back safely so if you leave him you will have to find him or hope he finds you.

H7: The goblins' dungeon

HELP: A window should be no obstacle to a thief with friends.
HINT: Who is the thief and who are his friends?
FURTHER HINT: Qvjgtu oca dg cdng vq tgcej yjgtg c jqddkv ecppqv.
EXTRA HINT: What would a pile of sand be doing in a dungeon?
FURTHER HINT: Jqy yqwnf aqw igv vjtqwij c yqqfgp fqqt ykvj pq mga?

H8: A big cavern with torches along the walls

HELP: You're doing fine.
HINT: The dungeon door must lead somewhere.

SECTION 4:

Beorn's House

Beorn's house lies on the edge of Mirkwood, and many locations can be explored from here.

H9: Beorn's house

HELP: You're doing fine.
HINT: Search carefully.

H10: The west bank of a black river

HELP: Boats can help. Look carefully.
HINT: If there is no boat on this side of the river, how would you get across?
FURTHER HINT: Yjcv yqwnf aqw wug vq rwnn vjg dqcv cetquu?

H11: Forestriver

HELP: You're doing fine.
HINT: The river is flowing very fast here.
FURTHER HINT: Fq pqv uyko vjku.

SECTION 5:
The Elven King's Halls

Here you must go through the Elven King's Halls to reach the last part of the game and retrieve the treasure.

H12: The green forest

HELP: You're doing fine.
HINT: The spider web is all that blocks your path.
FURTHER HINT: Urkfgtu nqqm chvgt vjgkt ygdu.

H13: A place of black spiders

HELP: You're doing fine.
HINT: Getting out of here presents the same problem as entering.
FURTHER HINT: Fq pqv yckv ctqwpf jgtg, dwv rncp aqwt gzkv ectghwnna.

H14: An elvish clearing with levelled ground and logs

HELP: You're doing fine.
HINT: A magic door will need magic to open it.
FURTHER HINT: Ikxg kv c vjqtqwij gzcokpcvkqn.

H15: The cellar where the king keeps his barrels of wine

HELP: Timing is critical. Remember barrels float.
HINT: What is beneath the trap door?
FURTHER HINT: Yjgtg ku vjg dwvngt rwvvkpi vjg dcttgnu, cpf jqy yqwnf vjku jgnr aqw?

17

H16: A dark dungeon in the Elven King's Halls

HELP: Wait around and time your exit carefully.
HINT: Take the advice.

SECTION 6:
Long Lake

L17: A wooden town in the middle of long lake

HELP: You're doing fine.
HINT: What does Bard do?

SECTION 7:
The Dragon's Desolation

This is the final section of the game. You must overcome the dragon, retrieve the treasure, and return home again.

H18: The halls where the dragon sleeps

HELP: A living dragon is deadly, look to Bard.
HINT: Bilbo is a very bad shot.
FURTHER HINT: Yjq jcxg aqw ogv dguv gswkrrgf vq mknn c ftciqp?

H19: A little steep bay, still and quiet, with an overhanging cliff

HELP: Wait a while.
HINT: Whose key will you need to use to open this curious door?

Part Three

A Tourist's Guide to Wilderland

Most of the game's locations are listed here and can be used for reference. The list is alphabetical, the location names in most cases being those which you will see when you first enter the location or use LOOK. This part of the book can be used as and when problems arise or routes must be chosen. Solutions given here are not always the only possible ones — there are often several ways in which a problem can be solved.

L1: Beorn's house

Here, if not already open, a curtain conceals a cupboard in which
some food can be found.

Enter:

—OPEN — Do this 0, 1 or 2 times until the cupboard is open.
—TAKE FOOD

EXITS:
NORTHEAST — the gate to Mirkwood (L20)
NORTHWEST — outside goblins' gate (L37)
SOUTH — the forest road (L16)
SOUTHWEST — a narrow dangerous path (L35)
NORTH — the great river (L23)

L2:   The bewitched gloomy place

EXITS:
WEST — the gate to Mirkwood (20)
EAST — the west bank of a black river (L48)

L3: A big cavern with torches along the walls.

The goblins' door seen inside the dungeon leads out here. It is invisible at first, but entering

—OPEN DOOR

reveals the door to the southeast. If you wish to go through you will have to do so immediately after opening the door, as it will shut by itself otherwise.

EXITS:
DOWN — the dark stuffy passage (L8)
NORTHEAST — the dark winding passage (L9)
SOUTHEAST — the goblins' dungeon (L22), through the goblins' door.

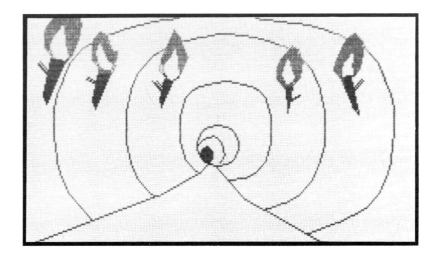

L4:   A bleak barren land that was once green.

Bard will stop here on the outward journey. From here he must continue north, and will not stop before reaching the dragon's lair.

To tell Bard which way to move, enter:

—SAY TO BARD 'NORTH'

EXITS:
NORTH — the ruins of the town of Dale (L40)
DOWN — a strong river (L43)

L5:   The cellar where the king keeps his barrels of wine.

This location provides a way through to the second half of the adventure, via the trap door. Going through is not an easy task, as below is the fast moving Forestriver in which you cannot swim. If you do not have the magic ring then the task will be made harder still as the butler may capture you. Consulting The Hobbit tells us that Bilbo and his partners escaped in a barrel. HELP confirms that you can do this — 'TIMING IS CRITICAL. REMEMBER BARRELS FLOAT.'

To aid your escape it is important that the butler does not see you, so remember to enter WEAR RING frequently or you must make sure you are in the barrel or through the trap door before you are seen and captured. If, as sometimes happens, you arrive to find the butler dead then you can't rely on him to throw the barrel through the trap-door. Your only solution then is to manage to get the barrel in the water and yourself on it.

To go through the trap door, enter:

—OPEN BARREL — if no barrel is visible then enter WAIT and try again.

—DRINK WINE — This only applies if there is some wine in the barrel, producing shome intereshting reshultsh!

—CLIMB INTO BARREL
—CLOSE BARREL — There may not be time to enter this, or the butler may close it himself.

—WAIT — Repeat this until the butler throws you into the water and you find yourself on the banks of Long Lake (L32)
If the butler sees and captures you at any point, wait to leave the dungeon (L7), wear the ring and try again. The butler follows a

24

fixed pattern of movement and studying this can provide clues as to the timing of your escape.

EXITS:
NORTH — the elven king's great halls (L11)
DOWN — Forestriver (L18), through the trap door.
NORTHEAST — A dark dungeon in the elven king's halls (L7), through the red door.

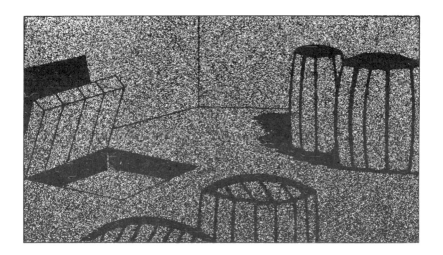

L6: A comfortable tunnel like hall.

This is Bilbo's house and the starting place of your adventure. The wooden chest here is the one into which you must put the dragon's treasure to complete the game.

On starting the game, you could enter:

—OPEN CHEST

Gandalf will almost certainly now open the round green door. If you wish to keep the curious map which he has given to you, go east now.

—EAST

You will then go through the round green door to the lonelands (L21)

If you wait and Gandalf himself goes east, you may meet him again and be subjected to one of his curious habits — a tendency to take the curious map, examine it, ask you what it is and finally return it to you, having wasted much of your time.

EXITS:

EAST — A gloomy empty land with dreary hills ahead (L21), through the round green door.

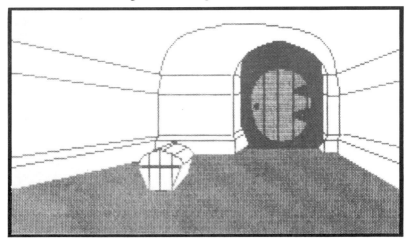

L7: A dark dungeon in the elven king's halls.

The clue to your escape is given by HELP — 'WAIT AROUND AND TIME YOUR EXIT CAREFULLY.' The butler unlocks and opens the door at regular intervals. It is best to be prepared, so when the red door is unlocked, wear the ring, if you have it, before leaving.

—WAIT — Repeat until the red door is unlocked.
—WEAR RING — The red door will now be opened.
—SOUTHWEST — To the cellar (L5).

The red door can be unlocked using the red key.

EXITS:
WEST — the elven king's great halls (L11), through the red door.
SOUTHWEST — the cellar where the king keeps his barrels of wine (L5), through the red door.

L8:   The dark stuffy passage

The network of dark stuffy passages go to make up the goblins' caves. The passages twist and turn making mapping difficult, so a list of possible routes has been included below. It is important to remember that these routes are not foolproof, so if you are captured at any stage leave the dungeon (L22) and continue using one of the routes from the dark winding passage (L9).

Route one:
From inside goblins' gate (L28) to get to the valuable golden ring —

—DOWN
—DOWN — If you do not see a goblin here then enter WAIT until one appears.
—NORTH
—SOUTHEAST
—EAST
—TAKE RING

Route Two:
From the dark winding passage (L9) to get to the valuable golden ring —

—SOUTHWEST
—DOWN — If you do not see a goblin here then enter WAIT until one appears.
—NORTH
—SOUTHEAST
—EAST
—TAKE RING

Route three:
From the small insignificant crack to get to the valuable golden ring —

—NORTHEAST
—SOUTHEAST
—EAST

Route four:
From the valuable golden ring to the underground lake —

—NORTH
—SOUTH
—WEST
—SOUTHWEST

Route five:
From the underground lake to Beorn's house (L1) —

—NORTH
—SOUTHWEST
—NORTH
—SOUTHEAST
—WEST
—NORTH
—DOWN
—SOUTH
—WEST
—EAST
—UP — Through the goblins' back door, which you may need to
open.
—EAST
—EAST

Route six:
From the valuable golden ring to Beorn's house (L1) —

—NORTH
—SOUTHEAST
—WEST
—NORTH
—DOWN
—SOUTH
—WEST
—EAST
—UP — Through the goblins' back door, which you may need to
open.
—EAST
—EAST

Route seven:
From the dark winding passage (L9) to Beorn's house (L1) —

—SOUTHEAST
—DOWN
—WEST
—EAST
—UP — Through the goblins' back door, which you may need to open.
—EAST
—EAST

L9:   The dark winding passage

The window here leads through to the dungeon (L22). To go through, Thorin will have to carry you.

EXITS:
SOUTHWEST — a big cavern with torches along the walls (L3).
SOUTHEAST — the dark stuffy passage (L8).

L10: The east bank of a black river

EXITS:
EAST — the green forest (L24)

L11: The elven king's great halls

-The red door to the east leads to the elven dungeon and is regularly opened and closed by the butler. To avoid capture if you intend to go south, wear the magic ring before actually moving.

To go through the magic door you will need to use the ring again:

—WEAR RING
—EXAMINE MAGIC DOOR
—WAIT — Repeat until the door opens.
—WEST — To go through the door.

EXITS:
SOUTH — The cellar where the king keeps his barrels of wine (L5).
EAST — A dark dungeon in the elven king's halls (L7), through the red door.
WEST — An elvish clearing with levelled ground and logs (L12), through the magic door.

L12: An elvish clearing with levelled ground and logs

From here you can go through the magic door, seen to the northeast, but to do so you must have the magic golden ring. This location is also a good place to leave Thorin, as from now on he will be more of a nuisance than a help.

To go through the magic door, enter the following:

—WEAR RING
—EXAMINE MAGIC DOOR
—WAIT — Repeat until the door opens.
—NORTHEAST — To go through the door.

EXITS:
WEST — The bewitched gloomy place (L2).
NORTHEAST — The elven king's great halls (L11), through the magic door.

L13: The empty place

Trying to go north from here produces the message 'The place is too full for you to enter'. See also L33.

EXITS:
SOUTH — A little steep bay, still and quiet, with an overhanging cliff (L30)
UP — the Lonely Mountain (L31)
NORTH — The empty place (see above).

L14: The forest

    EXITS:
    EAST — the waterfall (L47).
    WEST — the forest road (L17).

L15: A forest of tangled smothering trees

Again, the only exit is through the spider web. To go through, enter:

—BREAK WEB — Repeat if needed until the web is broken.

You should then go through before the web is repaired.

EXITS(all through the web):
NORTH — a place of black spiders (L38)
WEST — the green forest (L24)

L16: The forest road

From here you enter an area to be avoided, inhabited by creatures with pale bulbous eyes who will follow and kill you. To remain safe, return north.

EXITS:
EAST — the forest road (L17).
NORTH — the gate to Mirkwood (L20).

If you do see the pale bulbous eyes (and they see you) you can escape them by typing the direction you came from followed by WAIT, and then the directions again.

L17: The forest road

EXITS:
EAST — the forest (L14)
WEST — the forest road (L16)

L18: Forestriver

Southeast the fast river flows, but do not try to swim across as you will be swept forcefully against the portcullis and killed.

To look across the river, simply enter:

—LOOK ACROSS

EXITS:
NORTH — the mountains (L33)

L19: The front gate of the Lonely Mountain

If you meet the dragon here, don't panic! The dragon will not attack unless his treasure is taken. Bard has the task of actually killing the dragon, and should do so before you take the treasure.

EXITS:
NORTH — the halls where the dragon sleeps (L25).
SOUTH — the ruins of the town of Dale (L40).
WEST — the west side of Ravenhill (L49).

L20: The gate to Mirkwood

EXITS:
WEST — Beorn's house (L1).
SOUTH — the forest road (L16).
EAST — the bewitched gloomy place (L2).

L21: A gloomy empty land with dreary hills ahead

EXITS:
EAST — the trolls' clearing (L46).
NORTH — the trolls'clearing (L46).
NORTHEAST — a hidden path with trolls' footprints (L27).
WEST — a comfortable tunnel-like hall (L6), through the round
green door.

L22: The goblins' dungeon

Having been captured, the most obvious course of action is to try and escape. The door and window seem the most likely routes, but the door cannot be opened or smashed from this side and the window is too high to reach. HELP gives the clue — 'A WINDOW SHOULD BE NO OBSTACLE TO A THIEF WITH FRIENDS.'

You are the thief, a name Bilbo is called by the other characters in The Hobbit. Before escaping, however, there is a key hidden here which should be retrieved. To do this, enter the following commands:

—DIG SAND — This will reveal a trap door.
—BREAK TRAP DOOR — This may take a very long time. Repeat until the door breaks.
—TAKE KEY — This is the small curious key.

Thorin may take the small curious key himself, as it belonged to his father, Thrain.

To leave the dungeon, you must be carried through the window by one of the other characters. This can only be done if you are not carrying too much, so eating any food or lunch which you may have with you will help to reduce the amount which you are carrying.

—WAIT — This is only needed if no other character is present. Repeat until one enters.
—SAY TO THORIN 'CARRY ME' — Gandalf could do the same if Thorin is not present.
—SAY TO THORIN 'OPEN WINDOW' — Or Gandalf. Be careful as the window may already be open and Thorin will not respond.
—SAY TO THORIN 'WEST' — Through the window, into the dark winding passage (L9).

EXITS:
NORTH — a big cavern with torches along the walls (L3), through the goblins' door.
WEST — the dark winding passage (L9), through the window.

L23: The great river

EXITS:
NORTHEAST — the mountains (L33).
SOUTH — Beorn's house (L1).
EAST — the gate to Mirkwood (L20).
SOUTHWEST — a hard dangerous path in the Misty Mountains
(L26).

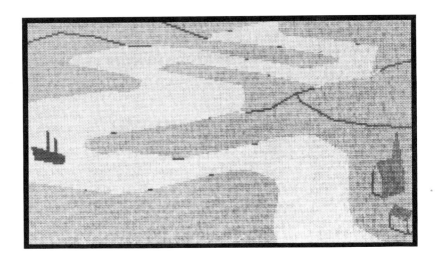

L24: The green forest

To the northeast is the spider web. To go through, enter:

—BREAK WEB — Repeat until the web breaks.
—NORTHEAST

EXITS:
WEST — the east bank of a black river (L10).
NORTHEAST — a place of black spiders (L38), through the spider web.

L25: The halls where the dragon sleeps

This room marks the end of your quest. Here you must take the treasure, but as soon as you do so the dragon becomes a threat. Wearing the magic ring is of no use as the dragon will burn everything in an attempt to kill you. For this reason the dragon must be killed, and Bard is the only one who can do this.

—WAIT — Repeat this until the dragon enters, or not at all if it is already here.
—SAY TO BARD 'SHOOT DRAGON' — Bard does his job.
—TAKE TREASURE

Now you have the treasure and must begin the return journey.

EXITS:
SOUTH — the front gate of the Lonely Mountain (L19).
EAST — a smooth straight passage (L42).
UP — the Lonely Mountain (L31).

L26:: A hard dangerous path in the Misty Mountains

EXITS:
WEST — Rivendell (L39).
NORTH — a narrow path (L34).
EAST — a narrow place with a dreadful drop into a dim valley (L36).
SOUTH — a narrow path (L34).

L27: A hidden path with trolls' footprints

North of here is the rock door, but no apparent means of opening it. HELP gives the clue 'A TROLLS DOOR NEEDS A TROLLS KEY'., the key needed being the large key to be found in the trolls' clearing.

Once you have the key, enter:

—UNLOCK DOOR
—OPEN DOOR

You can then go north through the door.

EXITS:
SOUTH — the trolls' clearing (L46).
NORTH — the trolls' cave (L45), through the heavy rock door.

L28: Inside the goblins' gate

This is the main entrance, leading down to the system of caves.

EXITS:
WEST, NORTH, SOUTH, EAST, SOUTHEAST, SOUTHWEST,
DOWN, NORTHWEST — a big cavern with torches along the
walls (L3).
NORTHEAST — the dark stuffy passage (L8).
UP — outside goblins' gate (L37), through the goblins' back
door.

L29: A large dry cave which is quite comfortable

This cave acts as a short cut into the goblins' caves, through the small insignificant crack. Waiting here reveals that the crack is regularly opened and a goblin steps out (probably capturing you!), then returns, closing the crack before repeating the process.
EXITS:
SOUTH — a narrow place with a dreadful drop into a dim valley (L36).
DOWN — the dark stuffy passage (L8), through the small insignificant crack.

L30: A little steep bay, still and quiet, with an overhanging cliff.

Here HELP returns the clue 'WAIT A WHILE'., and sure enough, having entered WAIT several times, a hole appears in the mountain side. This is the side door of the Lonely Mountain and can be unlocked using the small curious key found in the goblins' dungeon.

To go through the door:

—WAIT — Repeat until the door appears.
—UNLOCK DOOR
—GO THROUGH DOOR — Into a smooth straight passage.

EXITS:
SOUTH — the west side of Ravenhill (L49).
NORTH — the empty place (L13).
EAST — a smooth straight passage (L42), through the side door.

L31: The Lonely Mountain

EXITS:
DOWN — the halls where the dragon sleeps (L25).
WEST — a little steep bay, still and quiet, with an overhanging clitt (L30).
SOUTH — the front gate of the Lonely Mountain (L19).

L32: Long Lake

EXITS:
NORTH — a strong river (L43).
EAST — a wooden town in the middle of Long Lake (L50).
SOUTH — the waterfall (L47).

L33: The mountains

Trying to go east from here produces the message 'The place is too full for you to enter'. See also L13.

EXITS:
SOUTHWEST — the great river (L23).
SOUTHEAST — Forestriver (L18).
EAST — the empty place (see above).

L34: A narrow path

The narrow paths which run through the Misty Mountain are designed to mislead and confuse, leading round in circles or nowhere at all.

To retrieve the golden key hidden in the mountains, the following route can be used, starting and finishing at the Misty Mountain (L26):

—NORTH
—NORTHEAST
—NORTH
—SOUTHEAST
—DOWN
—DOWN
—DOWN
—DOWN
—EAST
—TAKE KEY — The golden key.
—UP
—WEST
—NORTH — Back onto the Misty Mountain

L35: A narrow dangerous path

EXITS:
EAST — Beorn's house (L1).
WEST — a narrow place with a dreadful drop into a dim valley (L36).

L36: A narrow place with a dreadful drop into a dim valley

EXITS:
EAST — a narrow dangerous path (L35).
WEST — a hard dangerous path in the Misty Mountains (L26).
NORTH — a large dry cave which is quite comfortable (L29).

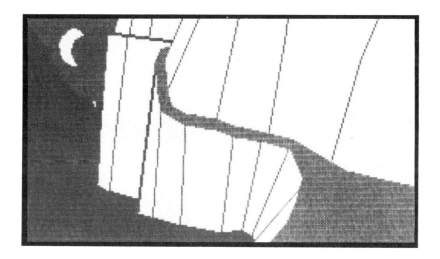

L37: Outside goblins' gate

The goblins' back door leads down into the goblins' caves. To open it, enter:

—OPEN

EXITS:
EAST — the treeless opening (L44).
DOWN — inside the goblins' gate (L28), through the goblins' back door.

L38: A place of black spiders

This is actually inside the spider web. To go through again, enter:

—BREAK WEB — Repeat if needed until the web is broken.

You should now go through before the web is repaired.

EXITS (all through the web):
EAST — the deep bog. Do not enter this location as you will sink into the bog and die.
WEST — the green forest (L24).
NORTH — an elvish clearing with levelled ground and logs (L12).
SOUTH — a forest of tangled smothering trees (L15).

L39: Rivendell

This is Elrond's home and he is usually to be found here. HELP gives the message 'ELVES ARE GOOD AT READING SYMBOLS', so Elrond can read the curious map for you.

It is important that you do ask Elrond to read the map, as otherwise the links between locations mentioned on the map will not appear in the game, and you may not be able to complete the adventure.

—SAY TO ELROND 'READ MAP'

Elrond will reply with one of several messages, which vary from game to game. These include:

'Go east from Long Lake to get to Lake Town'

'Go east from the forest gate to get to the bewitched gloomy place'

'Go north from Beorn's house to get to the great river'

'Go east from the Misty Mountain to get to a narrow place'

'Go west from the treeless opening to get to outside goblins' gate'

If you wait here, you will also receive some lunch:

—WAIT — Repeat this command until Elrond gives some lunch to you.

EXITS:
EAST — a hard dangerous path in the Misty Mountains (L26).
WEST — the trolls' clearing (L46). Do not go west until you are certain that day has dawned.

L40: The ruins of the town of Dale

EXITS:

NORTH — the front gate of the Lonely Mountain (L19).
SOUTH — a bleak barren land that was once green (L4).
WEST — the west side of Ravenhill (L49).

L41: The running river

On the return journey the wood elf should capture you either here or at the waterfall (L47). If the elf is not here, it is unwise to go west as this leads to the forest, where the pale bulbous eyes will stare at you . . .

EXITS:
NORTH — the waterfall (L47).
WEST — the forest road (L17)

If you do see the pale bulbous eyes (and they see you) you can escape them by typing the direction you came from followed by WAIT, and then the directions again.

L42: A smooth straight passage

EXITS:
WEST — a little steep bay, still and quiet, with an overhanging cliff (L30), through the side door.
EAST — the halls where the dragon sleeps (L25).

L43: A strong river

On the outward journey Bard will stop here. To continue, you must
both go up:

—SAY TO BARD 'UP'
—UP

EXITS:
UP — a bleak barren land that was once green (L4).
SOUTH — Long Lake (L32).

L44: The treeless opening

EXITS:

WEST — outside goblins' gate (L37).

EAST — Beorn's house(L1).

L45: The trolls' cave

Here you will find the short strong sword and the rope. To take both, enter:

—TAKE ALL

EXITS:
SOUTH — a hidden path with trolls' footprints (L27), through the rock door.

L46: The trolls' clearing

The less than friendly greeting the trolls give you here should alert you to their danger — you should leave immediately.

The hideous troll, however, is carrying the large key which you will need to help you continue the game. HELP provides the clue as to how you can take the key — 'WAIT FOR THE NEW DAY DAWNING'. Consulting the book The Hobbit at this stage reveals that trolls turn to stone in daylight, so you must leave and return once day has dawned.

One way of doing this would be:

—NORTH — Leave.
—WAIT — Repeat this until day dawns.
—SOUTH — Return to the clearing.
—TAKE KEY — Now that the trolls are harmless.

EXITS:
SOUTHWEST — a gloomy empty land with dreary hills ahead (L21).
SOUTHEAST — Rivendell (L39).
NORTH — a hidden path with trolls' footprints (L27).

L47: The waterfall

EXITS:
SOUTH — the running river (L41).
WEST — the forest (L14).

L48: The west bank of a black river

Here you must somehow cross the river. Swimming is of no use, as you will fall alseep in the mysterious waters and drown. In The Hobbit Bilbo used a boat and you, too, must follow this course of action, confirmed by HELP — 'BOATS CAN HELP. LOOK CAREFULLY'. No boat is visible, but enter:

—THROW ROPE ACROSS — Repeat until the rope lands in the boat on the other side of the river.
—PULL ROPE — The boat will glide across.
—CLIMB INTO BOAT — The boat will move by itself and carry you to the east bank (L10).
—CLIMB OUT

If Thorin is with you he can be left here. It would also be a help if at this point you do have the valuable golden ring, though it is not essential.

EXITS:
WEST — the bewitched gloomy place (L2).

L49: The west side of Ravenhill

EXITS:
NORTH — a little steep bay, still and quiet, with an overhanging
cliff (L30).
SOUTHEAST — a bleak barren land that was once green (L4)
EAST — the front gate of the Lonely Mountain (L19).

L50: A wooden town in the middle of Long Lake

Here you will meet Bard, who is carrying a bow and arrow. These seem ideal for shooting the dragon, but taking them is useless as you will find yourself to be a very bad shot. Bard himself is the key to the final stage of the game. Tolkein's novel tells us that it is he who shoots the dragon, and in order for you to succeed Bard must travel with you.

Fortunately, Bard moves only as instructed, but will keep moving in the same direction as long as he is able to. For this reason, it is important to send Bard in the right direction:

—SAY TO BARD 'NORTH'

EXITS:
NORTH, SOUTH, EAST, WEST — all lead to Long Lake (L32).

Index of Listed Locations

The locations detailed in the book are listed here in alphabetical order —
'L' before the location number refers to the third section, while 'H' means
that the location is also described in the second section.

Beorn's house	L1	H9
the bewitched gloomy place	L2	
a big cavern with torches along the walls	L3	H8
a bleak barren land that was once green	L4	
the cellar where the king keeps his barrels of wine	L5	H15
a comfortable tunnel like hall	L6	H1
a dark dungeon in the elven king's halls	L7	H16
the dark stuffy passage	L8	
the dark winding passage	L9	
the east bank of a black river	L10	
the elven king's great halls	L11	
an elvish clearing with levelled ground and logs	L12	H14
the empty place	L13	
the forest	L14	
a forest of tangled smothering trees	L15	
the forest road	L16	
the forest road	L17	
Forestriver	L18	H11
the front gate of the Lonely Mountain	L19	
the gate to Mirkwood	L20	
a gloomy empty land with dreary hills ahead	L21	
the goblins' dungeon	L22	H7
the great river	L23	
the green forest	L24	H12
the halls where the dragon sleeps	L25	H18
a hard dangerous path in the misty mountains	L26	H5
a hidden path with trolls' footprints	L27	H3
inside the goblins' gate	L28	

a large dry cave which is quite comfortable	L29	H6
a little steep bay, still and quiet, with an overhanging cliff	L30	H19
the Lonely Mountain	L31	
Long Lake	L32	
the mountains	L33	
a narrow path	L34	
a narrow dangerous path	L35	
a narrow place with a dreadful drop into a dim valley	L36	
outside goblins' gate	L37	
a place of black spiders	L38	H13
Rivendell	L39	H4
the ruins of the town of Dale	L40	
the running river	L41	
a smooth straight passage	L42	
a strong river	L43	
the treeless opening	L44	
the trolls' cave	L45	
the trolls' clearing	L46	H2
the waterfall	L47	
the west bank of a black river	L48	H10
the west side of Ravenhill	L49	
a wooden town in the middle of Long Lake	L50	H17

A GUIDE TO PLAYING THE HOBBIT

MELBOURNE HOUSE REGISTRATION CARD

Please fill out this page and return it promptly in order that we may keep you informed of new software and special offers that arise. Simply fill in and indicate the correct address on the reverse side.

Name ....

Address ....

.... Code ....

Which computer do you own? ....

Where did you learn of this product?

☐ Magazine. If so, which one? ....

☐ Through a friend

☐ Saw it in a Retail Shop

☐ Other. Please specify ....

Which magazines do you purchase?

Regularly: ....

Occasionally: ....

What Age are you?

☐ 10-15 ☐ 16-19 ☐ 20-24 ☐ Over 25

We are continually writing new material and would appreciate receiving your comments on our product.

How would you rate this software?

☐ Excellent ☐ Value for money
☐ Good ☐ Priced right
☐ Poor ☐ Overpriced

Please tell us what books/software you would like to see produced for your computer.

_____

_____

_____

PUT THIS IN A STAMPED ENVELOPE AND SEND TO:

In the United Kingdom return page to:

Melbourne House (Publishers) Ltd., Melbourne House, Church Yard, Tring, Hertfordshire, HP 23 5LU

In Australia & New Zealand return page to:

Melbourne House (Australia) Pty. Ltd., 70 Park Street, South Melbourne, Victoria, 3205.